HYPHEN THEATRE COMPANY PRESENTS

THE SOFT SUBJECT (A LOVE STORY)

BY CHRIS WOODLEY

Published by Playdead Press 2017

© Chris Woodley 2017

Chris Woodley has asserted his rights under the Copyright, Design and Patents Act, 1988, to be identified as the authors of this work.

A CIP catalogue record for this book is available from the British Library.

ISBN 978-1-910067-51-2

Caution
All rights whatsoever in this play are strictly reserved and application for performance should be sought through the author before rehearsals begin. No performance may be given unless a license has been obtained.

This book is sold subject to the condition that it shall not by way of trade or otherwise, be lent, resold, hired out, or otherwise circulated without the publisher's prior consent in any form of binding or cover other than that in which it is published and without a similar condition including this condition being imposed on the subsequent purchaser.

Playdead Press
www.playdeadpress.com

This production of *The Soft Subject (A Love Story)* was performed at Assembly Hall 3rd August - 28th August 2017.

Writer and Performer: Chris Woodley
Director: Amy Liptrott
Dramaturg: Anna Beecher
Designer: Agnes Wild
Producer: Esmé Patey-Ford and Chris Woodley
Assistant Producer: Jill Patterson
Stage Manager: Danica Corns
Photography: Olivia Hirst and Rianna Dearden
Artwork: Mihaela Bodlovic
PR: Talker Tailor Trouble Maker

Chris Woodley | Writer and Performer

Chris is an actor, writer and Co-Founder of Hyphen Theatre Company. Chris trained as an actor at Mountview Academy of Theatre Arts. As a writer his credits include: *The Soft Subject (A Love Story)* (Assembly Hall), *Bedtime Story* (Theatre Royal Stratford East), *Next Lesson* (The Pleasance) and Co-writer for *My Boyfriend Jesus Christ* (Karamel Klub) and *When The Lights Went Out at Christmas* (The BRIT School). His recent theatre credits include: *The Soft Subject (A Love Story)* (Assembly Hall), *My Boyfriend Jesus Christ* (Karamel Klub), *KATE* (Greenwich Theatre), *You Should Be So Lucky* (Above The Stag), *Walking: Holding* (The Yard), *From Russia, For Love* (Theatre Deli), *An Enemy of the People* (New Diorama), *The Gay Naked Play* (Above The Stag), *This Child* (The Bridewell Theatre) and *Rainman* (Karamel Klub). Television credits include: *Extras*.

Esmé Patey-Ford | Producer

Esmé is an actor and Co-Founder of Hyphen Theatre Company. Esmé trained as an actor at Mountview Academy of Theatre Arts. She made her West End debut in *Hand to God* at the Vaudeville Theatre. Other recent theatre includes: *Rituals to Mould her with* (Kings Place), *Myisi* (New Diorama), *Next Lesson* (Pleasance Theatre), *Asking Rembrandt* (Old Red Lion), *Oh, the Humanity and Other Good Intentions* (Tabard), *Games of Love and Chance* (Bedlam Theatre, Edinburgh Fringe), *Today I Bought a Yellow Car* (London Theatre Workshop) and *An Enemy of the People* (New Diorama). Television credits include: *Emmerdale* and *Coronation Street*.

Amy Liptrott | Director

Amy is a director, teacher and musician and studied for a Masters in Theatre Directing at Mountview Academy in London. As a director, her credits include: *The Falling* (24:7 Theatre Festival), *Contractions* (Mountview Academy), *Sour Nothings* (Tommyfield, Kennington), *Victor Frankenstein* (King's Arms, Salford), *Today I Bought a Yellow Car* (London Theatre Workshop), *Fringe Quartet* (Greater Manchester Fringe) and *Painted Arrows* (Iralm Fringe). Her co-directed work includes: *The Mermaid in the Gherkin Jar* (Northern Rose Physical Theatre Company). Her Assistant Director Credits include: *Neck of the Woods*, Dir. Douglas Gordon (HOME Manchester International Festival 2015), *Untold Stories*, Dir. Peter James (Old Laundry Theatre Bowness), *Duet for One and Separation* Dir. Elizabeth Newman (Bolton Octagon) and *Long Day's Journey into Night*, Dir. David Thacker (Bolton Octagon). Liptrott is also a dramaturge, a teacher and has extensive experience working with young people.

Anna Beecher | Dramaturg

Anne is a writer and performance maker. Her writing for theatre includes; *Nest* (artsdepot, Brighton Festival, Take Off Festival), *The Surplus* (Young Vic Taking Part) and *Living Things* (Battersea Arts Centre). Anna works widely as a dramaturg and is Associate Dramaturg for all female Shakespeare Company Smooth Faced Gentleman.

Agnes Wild | Designer

Agnes graduated from East 15 with a BA in Acting and Contemporary theatre in 2013. She is one of the founders of Lost Watch Theatre Company, with them she has directed three award winning shows; *Play for September*, *KATE* and *Own Two Feet*. Agnes directed the musical *Ronja* (National Theatre of Iceland) and assisted on the hit show; *The Heart of Robin Hood*. Wild is the founder of Miðnætti Theatre Company in Iceland.

Jill Patterson | Assistant Producer
Jill trained at Mountview Academy of Theatre Arts, Jill has a Masters in Performance and is an actor and director. As a director her credits include: *Kiki, The Queen of Montparnasse* (Catalyst and Bastille Festivals), *Coming Clean: Life as a Naked House Cleaner* (Camden People's Theatre and Brighton Fringe), *Catch Me* (Above the Arts Theatre), *Welcome to the Vox Box* (The Battersea Barge), *Why Not Us?* (Ugly Duck's Perform Gender Season), *My Boyfriend Jesus Christ* (Karamel Klub). Assistant Director credits include: *Pronoun/Chatroom* (Academy of Live and Recorded Arts). Her acting credits include: *Light Shining in Buckinghamshire* (The National Theatre), *A Declaration from the People* (The National Theatre), *A…My Name is Alice* (The Charing Cross Theatre).

Danica Corns | Stage Manager
Danica studied at Arts Educational Schools London and the National Youth Theatre and is an actress, producer and theatre maker. Corns is one of the founding members of Wonderbox; a female-led performing arts collective with whom she is currently working on *A Womb of One's Own*. Upcoming shows of *A Womb of One's Own* include The People's Republic of Stokes Croft, Bristol and The Space Theatre, London.

HYPHEN

Hyphen Theatre Company

Hyphen Theatre Company is a collaboration formed in 2013 between theatre makers Esmé Patey-Ford and Chris Woodley. We tell stories about recent history and make work that is honest, brave, playful and has heart. Shoreditch Town Hall has supported Hyphen since its inception, providing research and development, and rehearsal space in kind. We have also received similar support from The Pleasance Islington, Greenwich Theatre, Arts Depot and Above the Stag.

In response to Thatcher's Section 28, Chris wrote his first full-length play, *Next Lesson*. A sold-out industry preview was followed by a 6-night sold-out run in October 2015 at the Pleasance Islington. The show has since been workshopped in New York by an Anglo-American theatre company Cutting Hedge Productions. Chris then wrote his second full-length play, *The Soft Subject (A Love Story)*, which has been developed at Greenwich Theatre, Arts Depot and Shoreditch Town Hall.

Website: www.hyphentheatre.com
Twitter: @HyphenTC

Transforming mental health through research

About MQ

MQ is the UK's first major mental health charity focused on scientific research. We are working towards a vision of a world where mental illness is understood, effectively treated, and ultimately prevented.

Here's how we're doing it:

Improving understanding – by gaining more knowledge about how and why mental health conditions occur, we can speed up diagnosis, improve the search for better treatments, and find ways to prevent mental illness.

Improve current treatments – we believe everyone should have access to a mental health treatment that works for them. That's why we're working to get more people the right treatment, faster.

Prevent mental illness – some 75% of mental health conditions start before the age of 18, and can have lifelong impacts. Through research we can understand who is most at risk, and find ways to provide better treatments earlier – with the potential to transform lives.

We're delighted to see mental illness being given recognition in the arts, and works like *The Soft Subject* are playing a pivotal role in widening the discussion about this vital issue and how it affects us all.

Visit: www.mqmentalhealth.org to find out more and get involved.

ORINOCO FLOW: A NOTE FROM THE WRITER

It was way back in September 2015 me and my company partner Esmé did a reading of *The Soft Subject* crammed in her living room with wine, crisps and some amazing cast. I was hoping I'd written a blinder. Well, the script wasn't quite there, but there were some interesting ideas on a page. In January 2016 Hyphen Theatre Company were kindly given some space for rehearsal and development of *The Soft Subject* at Greenwich Theatre. Originally I'd written a show on the value of arts educations where three actor friends become frustrated drama teachers. The play was a fictional story, essentially about three people and transitional moments in their work and personal lives. Oooh edgy stuff, maybe, maybe not. The time working on the play at Greenwich had been incredibly valuable, but in terms of the sense of the story, it was real dogs breakfast.

On the final day at Greenwich, I took the team for a drink down the pub. The cast had been amazing and generous and beautiful with my words. However, as I strolled down the high street I couldn't help but have a 'worried Woodley' look on my face. Anna Beecher a good friend of mine was working on the project as a dramaturg, Anna sensed my unease. I was feeling a little lost and like this show might not go on. We stood on the street by the crossing waiting for the green man and she very sweetly and calmly said 'Chris, just decide what this play is about. What is it about? What is it *really* about?' It was such a strange moment for me as I knew in my heart exactly why I'd written it. I knew what it was but I hadn't quite told my head yet. My thoughts and feelings were waiting to catch up and buffer. It was that kind of a mixed feeling. Jittery denial.

A week later I was out on one of my long walks listening to my iPod, when suddenly I started crying. Uncontrollably. As I got to the park tears were pouring down my sweaty face. I was half listening to Enya and half wiping snot all over my arm. I couldn't stop crying. In a daze I'd stumbled across what the play was about over a chorus of Orinocho Flow. Sail away sail away sail way. I'd finally sailed away from a big chapter in my life. The story was there, and it felt like the time to tell it. To swim underwater and submerge myself in that amazing and difficult story, that drama lesson. It was about drama teaching and Ryan. The first big loves in my life.

So... I completely rewrote the show. It became autobiographical. I went solo, gulp. Oh and I extended the title by three words. *The Soft Subject (A Love Story)* Anna and I spent many sunny summer afternoons on the Southbank discussing ideas. She was so gentle with advice and always encouraged me to go deeper and to be brave. For that I'm so thankful, she pushed me to put truth on the page. Then in September 2016 we had the opportunity to fly to Iceland to work with a talented director Agnes Wild. Five days later, one cold Friday night in Rejakvik, I performed solo for the first time in my life to thirty strangers that knew nothing about me. That's how it rolls in theatre. It was bonkers. It was intense. It was also super sweaty. And it turns out in a solo show, it's always your bloody line. As the actor you don't need a highlighter pen, it is still you babe, acting, talking, more faces, try not to cry, oh now do the cry thing, do a slut drop, end on a song. All go home. The end.

But that isn't the end. It has been a whole extra year on top before getting it to this beautiful moment. So many people have contributed to the shows evolution. There is no such thing as a solo show. The show keeps changing, I'm sure it will continue to, I hope it does. I'd finally like to credit one more person for whom without their support, guidance and love I wouldn't be here, I genuinely believe that. James Pidgeon. The unsung hero in this show, you changed my life. Thank you for showing up at the right time, reminding me everything ends but more importantly the show goes on. I'll never ever forget that. Lots of love. Chris x

Dedicated to: The Woodley's

Acknowledgements:

James Pidgeon, Steve Strickland and Gary Wheeldon, Ric Watts, Simon Bedford, Shon Dale-Jones, James Haddrell, David Bryne, Helen Matravers, Simon Stephens, Sarah Goodall, Stuart Worden, Imogen Brodie, Sarah Niven, Anne Odeke, Olivia Hirst, Rianna Dearden, Kate Stirling, Loz Keystone, Chris Sherwood, Stanley Eldridge, Daniel Holme, Maria Turner, Lucy Wray, Hannah Barker, Bridgette Amofah, Sukh Ojla, Martin Casella, Tom Wright, Thomas Anderson, Eram Rizvi, Stac Dowdeswell, Katie Gonzalez-Bell, Neil Keats, Richard Morley, Beth Elliot, Rikki Beadle-Blair, John Gordon, Rhian Checkland, Alex Ramsden, Susanna Bennett, Kim O'Donoghue, Anna Maria-Nabirye, Ellen Verenieks.

Special thanks: The BRIT School, Birchwood High School, Queen Mary's University, Old Vic Lab, Lost Watch Theatre Company, The Bethlem Gallery, Talker Tailor Trouble Maker.

Supported by: Shoreditch Town Hall, Greenwich Theatre, Arts Depot and MQ.

Chris: black trousers, blue shirt, blue jacket, black shoes, black bow tie and glasses.

Chris stands at the door to welcome the audience. He asks them to fill up from the front row. On stage are three chairs and a briefcase. Wigfield's 1994 hit 'Saturday Night' plays. Chris moves centre stage. Music fades. Chris closes the door as he's speaking.

Keep it relaxed, breath, genuine.

CHRIS: I'm not an extraordinary person. In life we all have our own stories. Our own truth. Our own drama. It's choosing the right time. The right part. The right place. This is a true story. A love story.

Chris moves to centre stage.

> My story begins when I started my career as a teacher ten years ago. Yep, I'm a secondary school teacher. I don't teach the big subjects like Maths or Science. Not even English. (*Beat.*) I teach a gentler *softer* subject. Drama. Like right now... this is called a monologue. This is centre stage. This is called direct address. In any subject there are five parts to a lesson.

Pointing to his five individuals.

> Introduction. (*Beat*) Starter Activity. (*Beat*) Main Task. (*Beat*) Assessment of learning. (*Beat*) Evaluation.

Beat

> It doesn't sound very romantic does it? Maybe this is more of a love lesson? So, let's do this.

Chris opens the case.

Music: 'Jump Around' by House of Pain. Chris picks up the briefcase and places it on the chair. He takes out a placard that reads: 'The Soft Subject (A Love Story)'. He flips it over and it reads 'By Chris Woodley (me)'. Chris walks in front of the briefcase and to centre stage.

> Introduction. Introduce new ideas and get learners' attention.

He puts the cards away in the briefcase, slams it shut and spins around.

> WOW! *What a whopper!* (*Beat*) That was what the doctor said to my mum when I was born. He was talking about the size of my massive… *head.* Anyway, I wasn't planned. I was what my mum likes to call… 'a nice surprise.' I was born Christopher Michael Woodley on 19th May 1982, in Bromley, Kent. I was very nearly called Christian, but my uncle Dick told my dad that 'Christian was a poof's name'. (*Beat*) Interesting. You know what?

Walking upstage to the briefcase.

> I think people in glass houses called Dick shouldn't throw stones.

A moment with the case.

> This was my dad's. I decided to adopt it when I started my first job as a teacher. My dad, he's a Brazil nut trader. (*Beat*) I wouldn't be here if it wasn't for the Brazil nut. Yep. I'm deadly serious. He's shipped containers of Brazil nuts across the globe for decades. But yeah, my dad's 'a character'. I'm a character, he's a character. In this story we're all characters. Ultimately, he's a working-class boy done good. (*Beat*) My mum's more 'mild mannered', my dad's a cockney trader. Dad's a cross between Del Boy and Alan Sugar, but with a big heart. (*Beat*) "You're fired!! But no worries sunshine, there's job out there for you somewhere." My mum's a housewife who used to work for the General Phone Operator... hence my well-spoken voice.
>
> Mum and dad met at a dance in 1969 at The Hammersmith Palais one Saturday night. This is what was playing at the time:

Chris points and waits. Saturday Night *by Wigfield plays.*

> Nope. Actually this.

Chris stands silently. 'Lilly The Pink' by The Scaffold plays. Music fades. Chris nods.

> Yep. And nine months later dad proposed to her in The Griffin pub on Villiers Street. She was nineteen.

You might now know it as the Five Guys burger joint by Charing Cross station. Mum and dad have three brilliant kids. A boy, a girl - you don't need to know their names, and me. The dramatic one standing on stage.

I had an invisible aim when I was younger.

Goes to briefcase and gets out chalk. Chris writes 'To live happily ever after' says the words as he writes under his breath and cheeky clock to audience.

to live… happily, ever, after. Just like in the fairy-tales… and maybe that's why I was so drawn to this imaginary world of theatre. (*Beat*) A story. A drama. A moral.

Chris goes to sit crossed legged downstage centre.

I used to watch Disney's *The Little Mermaid* in the living room on repeat when I was a kid, while my dad was in the dining room watching Match of the Day. I've seen it well over thirty times. *The Little Mermaid* that is. Ariel, the mermaid is living, trapped under water… with a tail. She trades her beautiful voice for legs to be with the man she loves: Eric. Enter sea witch, a huge storm, true love, get married. Boom! And they all lived happily ever after.

Chris nods to the back. He stands.

> I made the huge assumption that by the time I was an adult, I could get married, have babies. I would wait for my Eric. One day my prince will come.
>
> You know that whole thing about Dick suggesting they don't call me Christian. Well, he'd only gone and bloody jinxed it. Just to be clear my loving parents couldn't give a shit who I sleep with. As long as I'm safe and happy. When I told my dad I had something important to tell him, his reply was (*Beat*) "Am I gonna need to record Match of the Day for this?" (*Beat*) Yes dad. Des Lynam's going to have to wait.

Chris takes the space downstage right.

> I spent most of my childhood at dance classes.

Chris performs a short musical burst of 'Macarena' by Los de Rio.

> That then turns into acting and dancing.

Chris performs a short burst of 'Go Greased Lighting'.

> That then turns into singing along to The Spice Girls and snogging boys in Soho by the time I'm thirteen.

Chris performs short second musical burst of 'Spice Up Your Life'. Music cuts.

> All good, clean, PG thirteen fun. (*Beat*) Well, ish.

Chris does cheeky wanking gesture.

> I wasn't massively mathematical or sporty at school. But, don't misunderstand me, my family are mathematical and sporty. My dad's been a keen marathon runner all his life. He's always told me.
>
> 'Life is a learning experience.'
>
> He runs marathons! My sister's a teacher. My brother's a trader, more like dad, happily married with kids. No nuts... I mean he has his own testicles. He works as a financial trader in New York. (*Beat*) I have *the* most incredible family. Does anyone really say that these days? Family is everything. (*Beat*) Like my sister, I trained as a teacher. And during my teacher training year something amazing happened to me. Me. Chris Woodley. Aged twenty-four. I fell in love.
>
> Not puppy dog love. Not crush love. Not kiss-me-behind-the-bike-shed love. Proper. Adult. Love.

Chris goes to briefcase and pulls out a photo, he looks at it, he gets lost in it for a moment. He doesn't reveal it to the audience.

> His name is... "Ryan."

He puts the photo back in the briefcase and snaps it shut.

> Starter Activity. Engage learners in activities that will feature in and inform the work in the main task. The first activity I'm going to introduce you to is

Still Image. Teaching often requires getting people to do things they don't want to do. Case in point:

He goes to his jacket and takes out two cards from his pocket.

I'd like two volunteers please. Nothing too scary. I'm going to give you a card and it will describe the Still Image I want you to create. Anyone?

Chris waits for two volunteers to offer themselves. He brings them to the stage.

On this card you each have the same description of a moment. I'm going to give you a slow countdown from three to create this Still Image. Just to remind you a Still Image is a still and silent. If you're not still, it's not a Still Image. Understood? Great.

Checks their understanding of what's on the cards.

The first still image represents how me and Ryan met. Three. Two. One. Frozen and still.

Chris hands them the first card that reads: "You are sitting in your own home, talking online to someone you fancy on a dating website." The two volunteers create this.

Fantastic. So you met online, lovely, nothing seedy. Less Grinder and more Guardian Soulmates if I'm honest. Now feel free to use the chairs. The second still image is what we did on the date. Three. Two. One. Frozen and still.

The second card reads: "You are sitting at a restaurant opposite one other, toasting with wine glasses". Chris walks to action pointing out 'Chris' and 'Ryan'.

> This is me and Ryan at dinner. It's Zizzi's. In Cambridge, Cambridgeshire. It's probably the most white working-slash-middle-class date you've ever witnessed. This next card is: how the date ended. Three. Two. One. Frozen and still.

Chris hands them the card that reads "You shake hands".

> Oh. Ok, well this isn't how it ended guys. (*Beat*) We've gone for a very West Wing ending haven't we? (*Beat*) And you've done *amazingly*. Can we have a round of applause for our volunteers?

Audience applause.

> It actually ended, outside the restaurant with a kiss.
>
> "Oi, you fucking poofs."
>
> Don't worry, we were fine, this is *not* a tale about homophobia: this is a love story.
>
> For the first time in my life, things felt right. Things were being brought to life. Suddenly I was the main attraction, the main part, suddenly I became centre stage and my life was in sync.

Chris moves centre stage.

After the first date I knew Ryan was 24, born in Surrey, and just like me, the youngest of three with an older brother and sister. Oooh, and his dad was a vicar.

If you want to find out the bigger, more personal stuff, you can use Hot-seating. Hot-seating is an activity used to find out more about the characters. Not in real life. In real life it takes about three months, seven Pizza Expresses, Summer Storm and three other International LGBTQ movies, a whole season of Dr Who and one fight. But the benefit of hot-seating is that it's quick.

Moves chair to centre. Takes off glasses.

CHRIS (AS RYAN): Hi. I'm Ryan Grove. I'm 24. I'm from Surrey. My greatest aspiration is to be the Cameron Mackintosh of the contemporary theatre world, but not a twat.

Not kissing Paul Taylor when I was fifteen at the church disco. Yes. That's my biggest regret.

Leans in.

Biggest… biggest secret? Ok. When I met Chris, I knew I was in love after the third date.

A fear? Chris will dump me for not being out to my parents.

Long beat.

CHRIS AS HIMSELF: Now, for future reference, Ryan's 6' 3", has brown hair, and blue eyes. (*Beat*) Tall, dark, handsome. Essentially Prince Eric. And also not out to his parents.

But, this not a coming out story, this is a love story.

Chris performs a sequence of actions to My Guy Mary Wells. We see him clock Ryan, the audience, then Ryan. Chris offers his hand. He turns into Ryan as if held in a dance. Chris does three step taps. Chris is twirled out. Chris goes into ballroom pose. Chris does three step taps in hold in a circle. Chris goes in kissing. The kissing is turned out to audience as a hug. Chris does three step taps. Chris dances next to him. Chris brushes Ryan off playfully. We see Chris pulled in. More kissing. Chris goes to the floor. Chris lays Ryan down. Chris stands up. Chris points to Ryan on the floor. Chris walks back casually. Chris mimes pulling off his top. Freezes.

CHRIS: *This* was a montage. An activity often used in drama to tell a story from fragments of pictures, text, or music. (*Beat*) Still Image. (*Beat*) Hot-seating. (*Beat*) Montage. All different tools to tell a story.

Chris sits on the chair stage left.

Not many other people know this but my dad loves a good old sing song in the car with me. He'd never admit that to his mates from football. Dad only uses one way to talk to me about my 'love life'. (*Beat*) In an email. When I'm at work. God, he loves a fucking email.

CHRIS (AS DAD): Dear Chris. How's you and that theatre producer fella Ryan? Love Dad. PS When do we get to meet him?

CHRIS (AS HIMSELF): Symbolic prop. Another tool to tell as a story.

Chris goes over to briefcase and pulls out a naked Eric doll. Music Aram Khachaturian's Adagio from Spartacus

CHRIS (AS RYAN): Chris?

Chris produces an Ariel doll. He walks the doll over to Eric.

CHRIS: Yes Ryan.

CHRIS (AS RYAN): All this travelling from Cambridge to Bromley South, what are we doing? Two nights a week together isn't enough.

CHRIS: I can come to Cambridge more.

CHRIS (AS RYAN): I know. I just want things to... I want things to change I guess. I want them to merge.

Chris puts Ariel's forehead to Eric's forehead and the dolls stare into each other's eyes.

We should move in together.

Silence.

You've gone quiet. (*Beat*) Why've you gone all quiet on me?

Silence.

CHRIS: Silence can be a good thing gorgeous.

CHRIS (AS RYAN): So?

CHRIS: So I think... I think it's the best fucking idea you've had in ages.

Eric doll moves towards Ariel. They kiss.

CHRIS (AS RYAN): You know what this means?

CHRIS: Er? It means we've doubled our CD collection?

CHRIS (AS RYAN): No. (*Beat*) I'm going to tell my folks. I'm going to do it.

CHRIS: Also, you're going to have agree to sleep on the correct side of the bed.

CHRIS (AS RYAN): You mean you want to sleep on *my* side?

CHRIS: No. I think you'll find it's always been my side.

CHRIS (AS RYAN): Oh really? Oh go on then. But you can buy the tickets for Robert Lepage next week.

CHRIS: Who the hell is Robert Lepage?

Chris places the Ariel doll on the case. Chris stands up holding the Eric doll, and takes it to the chair.

CHRIS: Ryan opens up my world to a whole new scene of theatre I'd never really known existed. More experimental. It's new. It's shiny. It involves Lyn Gardner reviews and hanging out at The Barbican, a lot. (*Beat*) Ryan adores my family. He gets drunk with us at weddings and we dance to *We Are Family* by Sister Sledge. He loves their truth. Now it was time to tell his family the truth.

'We Are Family' by Sister Sledge begins.

Chris walks over to the briefcase and pulls out a placard. It reads: 'This is a placard.' He flips it over and it reads: 'It's a way of reporting facts.' Chris pulls out another placard: 'Ryan came out.' He flips it over: 'His parents understood.' Chris pulls out another placard that reads: 'His dad, who's a vicar, said...' Chris flips over the placard: 'We are all God's children.' He pulls out another placard that reads: 'My dad sent an email that said...' Slams briefcase as music cuts.

CHRIS (AS DAD): Dear Chris. Big family Christmas in NYC? Love Dad. PS bring your fella.

Chris appears wearing a little Christmas hairband. Home Alone Music?

It's Chriiiiistmas! Can you tell? (*Points*) *Symbolic costume.* Me, mum, dad, my sister and Ryan fly to New York to spend it with my brother and his wife. All together as one big family. Dad couldn't be more chuffed. (*Beat*) There was much excitement in the family as my nephew was on the way, and I spent much of Christmas Day feeling my sister-in-law's belly. 2007 will *always* be the Christmas of family, and love.

Walks to chair as subway.

Boxing Day.

Chris sits.

Ryan and I catch the subway – he wants to take me to Christopher Street. It's December. It's freezing. It's snowing. Well, it's sleeting.

We reach the corner of Christopher Street and he stops. Standing on the sidewalk I look up at the sign at the cross roads. *It's where Christopher Street and Grove Street meet.* (*Beat*) Ryan pulls me in close, giving me the biggest hug.

CHRIS (AS RYAN): Christopher will you marry me?

CHRIS: What?

CHRIS (AS RYAN): Will you marry me?

Chris nods. He laughs.

CHRIS: Yes, Ryan Grove… Yes, of course I'll marry you.

Chris does dramatic turning to the back kissing gesture. Christmas Time (Don't Let The Bells End) by The Darkness begins.

> Ok. Ok, the kissing wasn't that dramatic. But the question was very simple. The answer was very clear. (*Beat*) Flash forward to two hours later. It's midnight. Ryan's asleep. The huge borrowed apartment we are in is completely empty. (*Beat*) Oh, except for the inflatable mattress we're sleeping on.

Chris walks forward to the apron/edge of the stage.

> Floor to ceiling windows and no blinds. The New York skyline is a buzzing orange plasma screen. I get up, trying not to wake my future husband. I walk to the window. It's the most incredible view of the Hudson River and I can see the Statue of Liberty far away in the distance. I'm stark bollock naked and I'm not alone. I'm not alone.

Chris looks up to Ryan doll on briefcase.

> Our location is next to ground zero. I can see the huge construction site with bright orange floodlights and movement visible below. I've never felt so high.

Chris puts the Eric doll away quite abruptly.

> In the morning... something had shifted. I was more in love with Ryan than ever. We looked down at the construction site below us.

Chris walks towards to front of stage. He talks as if Ryan is behind him.

Shouldn't we wait and buy a house first?

Turns around to Ryan

I just think. Shouldn't we wait and buy a house?

I wanted to marry Ryan, but I wanted other things too. If we were going to spend fifteen thousand pounds to mark our love and dedication, well wouldn't it be better off spent on bricks and mortar? A home of our own. Ryan smiled. He kissed me.

Chris nods as Ryan.

Chris takes off symbolic hairband and puts it in the briefcase.

Winter came and went. Spring sailed by. And by Summer my nephew was born. Brandon Christopher Woodley.

Chris moves from the chair to centre stage.

It's August. I'm spending a month working with Ryan at The Edinburgh Fringe on a show called *Story of a Puffin*. It's my first experience of Edinburgh. Ryan's producing the show! I'm... flyering.

Chris gets flyers out of briefcase and flyers the front row.

But I'm on such a high, I'm not even phased about the prospect of the GCSE Drama results coming out. Some of the student devised work was well... it was shit. (*Beat*) His show *Story of a Puffin*... well. IT WON A FRINGE FIRST! It was a wonderful moment for him. Well, for both of us. (*Beat*) And with a euphoric high comes...

Crescendolls by Daft Punk plays. Chris dances in celebration until phone rings.

Oh, and here's another theatrical device to move the story forward.

Hi mum! I wasn't sure when dad was getting in from Brazil so I haven't called (*Beat*) (*Beat*) No I'm listening, go on. (*Beat*) So dad's... (*Beat*) Do you want me to fly home? (*Beat*) OK (*Beat*) Once they put the stent in the heart, what next? (*Beat*) Sure, you go. (*Beat*) Yes, call me then. Ok. Send my love to dad. Tell him I love him. I love you.

Long silence. Chris takes in the moment.

Chris puts his mobile back in his pocket. He walks forward towards the audience.

You carry on with the show. You carry on with the performance.

Don't worry, dad didn't die. He's a tough nut. This is not a tale about bereavement. This is a love story. (*Beat*) But it was a long recovery, so the emails came in thick and fast.

CHRIS (AS DAD): Dear Chris, how's Ryan? Dear Chris, how's school? Dear Chris, keep calling ya muver won't you?

CHRIS: Sometimes at school I have some hard days. Schools can be full-on, you know? If something's going on in your personal life, it's hard to turn up and plaster on a smile. Kids see through that shit. When you're in pain they can hear it in your voice. The way you take the register. The way you write the date on the board. But any pain I experience, Ryan is never the cause. He plays music in the kitchen and does that adorable bum wiggle to get me to stop crying.

Aim: To live happily ever after.

Main Task. (*Beat*) The main part of the lesson where the learning takes place in order to achieve the aim.

It's 2009. (*Beat*) We've bought a house. A beautiful little terrace in the heart of Cambridge. And when I say beautiful, I mean it looks like the seventies have thrown up on it... everywhere. Wood chip on every single wall. A hideous staircase that doesn't meet building regulations. This shitty green carpet. The avocado bathroom is tiny and covered in lime-scale. It's fucking vile. I love it. I love it because it's ours. Our own little bubble. Of course we're going to redecorate. We're going to change it and make it good. And that's not the only change. You are now looking at... Chris Woodley: Head of Drama.

Chris does a high kick.

> Dad's so proud. He sends me an email that says 'Proud' in the subject heading.
>
> We tend to the garden. We have dinner parties. We pay the mortgage. I actually quite like paying the mortgage. Ryan does *all* the cooking. He sorts the bills. He calls Virgin Media about their appalling service. I do the washing, the cleaning, I answer the door to Jehovah's Witnesses. We both have roles to play. We're happy in our little bubble.

CHRIS (AS RYAN): Chris, it's raining out... do you want an umbrella?

Chris moves to one side. Clocks Ryan. The audience. Clocks Ryan. Smiles back at the audience.

CHRIS: It's 2010. Life is sweet. Disney on repeat. Nothing to report. In fact, if this was a school report is would just say, 'A sound effort. Keep up the good work.'

Chris hands audience member on the front row a paper report.

> So it's 2011.

Hands sheet of paper out.

> And it's my fifth year of teaching.

Hands sheet of paper out.

> Second year as a Head of Drama.

Hands sheet of paper out.

>Something's not quite right.

Hands sheet of paper out.

>But I can't quite pin-point what it is.

Hands sheet of paper out.

>I'm enchanted by my magical kingdom.

Hands sheet of paper out.

>My fairy-tale ending.

Hands sheet of paper out.

>But I'm disenchanted by teaching.

Hands sheet of paper out.

>I like the staff.

Hands sheet of paper out.

>I have the most incredible GCSE group.

Hands sheet of paper out.

>However, all the paperwork is killing me.

Hands sheet of paper out.

>The higher up the ladder I get.

Hands sheet of paper out.

> The less time I'm spending on the shop floor.

Hands sheet of paper out.

> The repetition is suffocating.

Throws the rest of the paper up in the air.

> Sir what's multi-role?

Clocks right.

> Sir what's visualisation?

Clocks left.

> Sir why do we use silence?

Clocks right.

> Sir what is repetition?

Clocks left.

> Sir what is repetition?

Clocks left.

> So we're in Cambridge in a lovely restaurant. It's our favourite.

Chris moves a single chair.

Ryan, I just feel like sometimes, I'm not teaching them about the purpose of theatre. It's a tick-box exercise of ingredients. Right class, your work must include the following elements... ...I can't watch fucking *War Horse* anymore. It makes me want to poke my eyes out.

(*Beat*)

Do *not* suggest *Woman In Black*. Do *not* say it! (*Beat*) I just don't want to read another fucking GCSE review, reducing a piece of art to marks out of forty. Do you know you need 97% in Drama to get an A*? And they call it the soft subject. My first year of teaching I took the kids to see a DV8 show, it was about sexuality. It really-

(*Beat*)

Yeah it moved me! (*Beat*) The next day the other Drama teacher comes up to me and she's like...

Chris stands up and folds arms.

CHRIS (AS OTHER TEACHER): Oh my god have you heard?

CHRIS: What?

CHRIS (AS OTHER TEACHER): About last night on the train babe?

CHRIS: No. What?

CHRIS (AS OTHER TEACHER): Callum Edwards.

CHRIS (DIRECT ADDRESS): Oh shit. What's happened? Schools are really picky about how students get home from the theatre now. I'm thinking, he's been mugged, he's been stabbed, he's been trampled by Joey the horse in a cruel twist of fate because I didn't take the class to see *War Horse*. My teaching career flashes before my eyes. I'm dead. No, *he's* dead.

CHRIS (AS OTHER TEACHER): No. He's gay. He's gay babes. He came out on the train.

Chris: Oh right.

Beat. RUSH TO THE CHAIR.

CHRIS (TO RYAN): Ryan, on the train he said "I've never seen a show like that. I think those people are really brave for telling their story. Their honesty really moved me. So I'm going to be brave. I'm gay." Callum can't write about drama for shit. But, he felt something. He was moved.

Silence. He stands.

CHRIS: Visualisation. This is an activity where everyone needs to close their eyes. Right everyone. Let's do that. (*Beat*) Everyone close your eyes. Go on. I'll tell you when to open them.

Chris waits for audience members to close their eyes.

It's 2011. (*Beat*) You're not you. You're someone else. You're Ryan, walking down your street. It's night-time. Victorian terraced house after Victorian terraced house. You've been away working for the best part of December, and after a fleeting visit to your parents' for Christmas with Chris, you're on your way home together. It's raining. In one hand you are holding an umbrella, in the other you've got a large suitcase. Chris is striding ahead of you. Always rushing ahead. He's keen to get home and watch the new Danish TV phenomenon *The Killing*. (*Beat*) The living room is dark as you enter.

Chris rushes to the Christmas tree and switches on the lights. You put the case down. Sit on the sofa. You notice all the unwrapped presents still under the tree. *Finally, you're home.* Chris is coming towards you with a big smile on his face. He's so smiley. He's making that smiley face. He sits next to you and places his hand on your hand. It's surprisingly warm. He places his other hand gently over your eyes to close them. His hand on your face is soft. He's got something to tell you. Chris says:

Chris picks out Christmas hairband from briefcase.

>Don't open your eyes. I just want to say… these last few weeks with you gone have really taught me something. (*Beat*) I've *never loved anyone* as much as I love you. I want to grow old with you. I want to spend the rest of my life with you. (*Beat*) I want you

> to be the man that holds my hand after I've put the kids to bed. I love you Ryan. You can open your eyes now. Open them. Will you marry me?

Lights come back on. Chris stands smiling. Wide-eyed and bushy-tailed. A silence. His face turns from excitement to uncertainty and he slowly pulls off the hair band.

Silence.

> I don't understand. (*Beat*) Enter sea witch.

Chris stands and takes a moment. Take it in.

> The rest I don't remember. I didn't shed a tear. Not one. That would be later. That night I didn't sleep. Have you ever lain in bed at night next to someone you love? Watched them knowing something they've said has changed your life forever? And now they're sound asleep, far away in the land of nod. I was wide awake.
>
> We're two spoons in a dark draw. I lie looking at the curtain with my back to Ryan. I watch it the whole night as it turns to day. The first person I call? Strangely it's my brother in New York. I *never* call him. Ever. He *always* calls me. It's 7am in the UK and 2am in the US.

Chris walks over to a chair stands. He gets out his phone.

CHRIS (AS BROTHER): Hello?

Beat.

Bruv? You alright?

Chris sits.

Chris?

CHRIS: I lose my shit. I mean I completely lose it. I'm trying to talk and all my brother can hear is this elongated wail, one long guttural cry. I can't get a word to form in my mouth to speak.

CHRIS (AS BROTHER): Chris?

Chris tries to form a word in his mouth to speak. Can't find the word or breath.

CHRIS (AS BROTHER): Calm down.

Chris tries to form a word in his mouth to speak. Can't find the word or breath.

CHRIS (AS BROTHER): Just calm down.

Chris tries to form a word in his mouth to speak. Can't find the word or breath.

CHRIS (AS BROTHER): Talk to me mate… please. Chris?

Chris tries to form a word in his mouth to speak. Can't find the word or breath.

CHRIS: At some point later when time has passed my brother recounted the horror of receiving this phone call. He thought our parents were dead. He thought dad had had another heart attack.

Re-calibrating the main task. Must be open to adapting lesson plan!!

Must remember Aim: To live happily ever after.

I couldn't go to work. I felt it wasn't real. Teaching *Romeo and Juliet* to a bunch of pissed off school kids. Like I was on the outside of my classroom watching a group of kids figure out their roles and the stage directions without me.

Chris stands.

Stage directions. (*Beat*) Stage directions are instructions for the actors.

I'd like two volunteers again please.

Chris picks a member of the audience, brings them to the stage.

I'd like you to sit here with your back to the audience and follow the stage direction. I'd like to you to play Chris. I'm going to play my sister.

Chris places the other audience member on a chair.

You are going to read the stage direction that are highlighted, at a steady pace.

Audience member reads: Chris's sister sits next to him. She takes Chris's hand. She smiles. Chris doesn't smile. His sister smiles again. Chris looks away. His sister tries to speak. She pauses. His sister doesn't know what to do. She begins to cry. She begins to cry because she's hurting for him and doesn't know what to say. She doesn't know how to make it better. She can't.

CHRIS (AS SISTER): I'm so sorry darling. I'm so sorry. (*Beat*) It will pass. This feeling. It's a cliché. But this feeling will pass.

Audience member reads: Silence. Chris looks towards his sister.

CHRIS (AS SISTER): School called me darling, this morning. Everyone wants you back. The school says when you're ready you should come in, just for an initial meeting. Maybe we can go in a couple of weeks. I mean, after things settle.

Thank you both for your help with this particular bit of the story. If you'd like to go back to your seats that be great. Didn't they do well.

CHRIS: As a teacher I've got really good at reading stage directions. Always the stage directions never the Juliet.

We often forget about the others caught in the cross fire. *(Long beat)*

> I use an expression a lot in the coming weeks: 'I just want to opt out'. Do you want me to call school? Do you want some dinner? Dad says you should go for a walk? 'I just want to opt out'.

Chris walks over to the briefcase.

> It's New Year's Eve. I'm sat in the tiny room in the house that Ryan and I have built from nothing. (*Beat*) Well, built from love. I'm sat on the floor.
>
> My sister is sitting on the bed nervously rubbing her foot into a crack in the floor board. These beautiful dark varnished stained floor boards. I'd helped choose the colour over the phone during a hurried break time, almost three years ago.

Chris, while sitting on the floor, takes placards from the briefcase and places them on the case. The first placard reads 'Subtext.'

CHRIS (AS SISTER): Chris are you sure you want to be here on New Year's Eve? Why don't you want to come back to mum and dad's? You look so tired darling.

Chris pulls out placard that reads: Sister: 'I don't want you to stay here'.

> Why don't you come see mum and dad yeah? You need to eat.

Chris pulls out placard that reads: Sister: 'We want you where we can keep you safe.'

> I just don't want anything to happen when I'm not here Chris.

Chris pulls out placard that reads: Sister: 'What if you kill yourself?'

> I don't want to go home to mum and dad. (*Beat*) Then something... happen... and have to explain to them I couldn't convince my little brother to come home. Please Chris. You don't look yourself. What if something happens and I'm not here.

Chris pulls out placard that reads: Sister: 'I don't want you to kill yourself?'

> Chris I need you to promise.

Chris pulls out placard that reads: Sister: 'I love you'.

A verse of Auld Lang Syne (rock/techno version)

Chris takes it in. He takes a breath. Puts the placard in the briefcase. He moves the briefcase to the side of the chair. He sits. Music begins to fade slowly.

CHRIS: Going to the doctor's is painful. My sister playing 'big sister' when I'm nearly thirty years old.

Chris shifts toward other chair as if talking to doctor.

CHRIS (AS DOCTOR): Now Chris, we *have* to ask this question. Have you had any thoughts of hurting yourself or others?

CHRIS (AS SISTER): Would you like me to leave the room darling?

Chris looks at the other empty chair. Shakes his head at sister.

CHRIS (AS DOCTOR): Have you had any suicidal thoughts?

Chris looks at doctor. He pauses. Chris shakes his head.

CHRIS: Did I have thoughts? Yes. I'd contemplated it. The thing is I'm a complete wimp. (*Beat*) It would have been a long hot bath. Sleeping tablets and a bottle of gin.

Narrating. Narrating is what you do when you're giving a spoken commentary on the action taking place during a drama. It's a useful technique when you want to inform an audience what's happening.

(Framing of the narrating. Puppets of Ken doll finding Ariel/ drifting apart)

I imagined Ryan finding me. Me, deep below the bath water. We didn't even have a lock on the shitty bathroom door. We couldn't afford to do the house up all in one go. The bathroom was going to be done last. But then what? I'd be dead. Ryan would feel like shit for the rest of his life. And my mum and dad would never sleep again.

There's a sense of a dark cloud hanging in the air. Not just at our Cambridge postcode, but I can feel it around me. The sense of loss when foundations are broken. Unmet expectations from friends, family and loved ones. Ryan will not be the brother-in-law you'd hoped for. Chris will not be the father to the grandkids you so want. (*Beat*) But we're all alive. Sometimes that was the hardest bit. Being alive. (*Beat*) My best friend Anna lost her boyfriend of six years to cancer. However, she was the first to come to me, hold my hand and say 'death is simpler than separation'. It offers closure and a cleaner ending. She meant every word. (*Beat*) People offering that 'there are plenty more fish in the sea' is dangerous for a man that can't remember to swim.

If I had told the doctor my thoughts, I'd probably be sectioned. I couldn't let that happen. It's not a great addition to a teacher's CV. (*Beat*) I went to therapy. Her name was Helen. She looked a bit like Olivia Coleman on a really good day, when she's about to win a BAFTA. Every Monday at 4pm I went to Helen's house. It was a ten-minute walk from where we lived. You weren't allowed to arrive early, that was important. There was nowhere for you to wait. You had to arrive on time.

Chris stands. Gets Dictaphone.

I stood outside looking at my phone, watching the minutes. 3:59. 3:59. 3:59. (*Beat*) 4:00.

Chris sits on the chair. He sits with his feet on his left side as Helen. He's leaning back.

CHRIS (AS THERAPIST): What would you like to ask Ryan?

Chris shifts in his chair forward. Taking to Ryan.

CHRIS: Why don't you love me anymore?

Chris shifts in his chair into Ryan pose.

CHRIS (AS THERAPIST): And have you asked him?

CHRIS: (*To Audience*) Ryan said... he's wasn't sexually attracted to me anymore.

Chris moves to centre talking to audience.

> He was saying the magic had gone. (*Beat*) He'd loved the magic trick. But he'd seen the trick before. Countless times. From the front, from the back, the sides, with the lights on and off and now... The magic's gone. He will always see the hidden string, the fake screen or the marked card.

(Little Mermaid giving up her voice to find a voice. The lack of my magic means I've found my voice again. Magic quotes. Sea witch's magic. Chris and Ryan identity I just don't know who I am anymore.)

Chris gets up, does a 'shall I sit here?' look, and walks nervously over to the left chair.

> I'm Chris Woodley. My classical speech is *The Life and Death of King John*. Playing Arthur.

Chris sits.

> Have you the heart? When your head did but ache,
>
> I knit my handkercher about your brows,
>
> The best I had, a princess wrought it me,
>
> And I did never ask you for it again
>
> And with my hand at midnight held your head,
>
> And like the watchful minutes to the hour,
>
> Still and anon cheer'd up the heavy time,
>
> Saying, 'What lack you?' and 'Where lies your grief?'

End scene face. Chris stands.

> There's something I forgot to tell you. This is where I drop a teeny, tiny, bombshell. Not personal. But professional. Before Ryan *threw* a grenade into my home I'd secretly been wanting to go back to acting. To drama school. Just think of it as a sub-plot that's been incredibly quiet and not discussed up until this point. I'd already made the application before *my personal apocalypse.*

Chris gestures to show the scale of the apocalypse.

> Auditioning was interesting. I was so broken by then if you'd asked me to do anything, I would have

done it. Be a sausage in a pan, take a shit on stage... not that I did.

Chris walks to the other chairs and stands in front.

> And back at work I feel like the understudy for my own life. I mean the show goes on. But I'm stuck, trapped... in a room. Hearing the usual voices somewhere close by. *How you feeling? Is there anything I can do? I'm so sorry.* I'm not giving my best performance in front of the kids. Kids can be amazing. (*Beat*) Kids can also be cunts.

Chris stands switching left and right, as various students.

CHRIS (AS STUDENT): Sir, not to be disrespectful, but you've been off for ages. Sir I'm not being funny or anything, sir, but were you sick? Sir, what does disentangle mean? Sir, why does Romeo kill himself over Juliet? Sir, why can't we see *War Horse*? Sir, are you leaving?

CHRIS: In the staffroom I hear this expression: *don't let it define you Chris. Chris don't let this-*

> Yes, thanks! Look, I've got to get ready to teach Year 12 about Verbatim Theatre so...

Chris gets out his mobile phone.

> I get a text. I get a text. And it reads like this, word for word.

CHRIS (AS RYAN): Chris. I've got the latest from the solicitor re the sale of the house. I've asked them if we need to sign together. On the stairs front, he's suggesting we buy a £75 indemnity insurance policy that would cover us if the stairs don't meet building regulations. It pains me slightly to do this, I think we should go ahead with this just to keep the wheels moving. Let me know what you think. Ryan. Kiss.

Take it in.

CHRIS: Ryan and I are living in the house as the months pass. Separate rooms under one roof. Six years sleeping on one side of a bed. Where's my side gone? Going to bed alone. Getting up alone. Where's my side gone? My side's next door, in the spare room, sleeping on his side. Separated by a wall once covered in wood chip that we'd stripped and painted. Our parents coming to help, endless cups of tea, sitting on dust sheets watching the plaster dry. Hand-me-down items from our parents' lives that made it into our home. We made this house a home and soon it was going to be someone else's.

The day mum and dad came to collect my stuff is blurry. It was the first physical stage of separation. Their car pulled up outside and I could see my parents stop for moment before they got out and I felt the complete and utter sense of failure. Dismantling this beautiful house. Things were already in boxes. Dad lifted the heavy items and mum attended to cleaning upstairs. Dad was in a zone. This was standard dad. Everything done at speed and with military precision.

CHRIS (AS DAD): The faster we pack the boxes the less pain my son will be in; the faster we pack the boxes the less pain my son will be in; the faster we pack the boxes the less pain my son will be in…

The table. The quilt. The mirror… *Shit.* The mirror.

Chris stands as his dad.

What is it Chris?

What?

You haven't decided who gets to keep it. Oh. Ok. Well?

Silence. Chris smiles.

CHRIS: As wanky a metaphor as it is… my dad stood by the car holding a giant mirror up to me. Reflecting me right back. Behind me I could see the empty shell of a home.

CHRIS (AS DAD): Ok son. Look, here's the thing. If I stand here any longer, if I stand still watching you… I'm going to cry. I know this is hurting you, but believe me it's hurting me and your mother just as much, because we love you and we hate to see you in pain. So… the mirror? (*Beat*) I'm gonna put it in the car.

CHRIS: I'd never seen my dad cry.

Silence.

> Ryan and I spent one more night in that house. In the morning it was raining. And not just raining. Or pouring. It was a summer storm. It was raining like it had never rained before on our little house. The rain pouring down the paths we'd walked. I hoped the rain might clean the streets, or even clean the pain away. (*Beat*) I won't share our last conversation. But the last thing he said to me was…

CHRIS (AS RYAN): Chris, do you want an umbrella?

Chris stands. CHANGE IN TONE. HIGH ENERGY.

CHRIS: It's 4th July 2012. (*Beat*) Independence Day. The night of our school's talent show. I'm off stage while my favourite Year 9 student is happily doing her cheer-leader routine to Carly Rae Jepsen's *Call Me Maybe*.

Chris starts a high energy cheer-leader routine to Carly Rae Jepsen's Call Me Maybe. *During this time, he moves over to briefcase. First placard reads "Text from Ryan. Chris pulls out another larger placard; it reads "The house has been sold." He flips over the placard: "All the best with the show. Rx" Chris goes back to dancing on stage. Chris takes a moment. Chris goes back to briefcase; he pulls out a placard which reads: "£50,000 in my bank account." He turns it over: "Still… money can't buy love." Chris packs items and is lost in thought. Music ends.*

CHRIS (AS STUDENT): Sir, you ok?

CHRIS: Yeah.

CHRIS (AS STUDENT): You sure sir?

CHRIS: Yeah.

Beat.

CHRIS (AS STUDENT): Ok. (*Beat*) I'm *so* excited tonight, my dad's in the audience.

CHRIS: I bet he's really proud. Go see him.

CHRIS (AS STUDENT): I will. I'm... I'm really sad you're leaving you know sir. (*Beat*)

CHRIS: Yeah? Yeah... I'll miss this. But, things change.

CHRIS (AS STUDENT): I really wanted to get you for GCSE Drama... But I guess not eh?

CHRIS: I'm sorry. (*Beat*) It's really what *you* do with it that counts. You'll be amazing.

CHRIS (AS STUDENT): I'm not going to lie, you're pretty strict sir, but at least people know they can't piss about in your lesson.

    Shall I go sir? I can wait with you for the next act if you want?

CHRIS: No. That's ok. Off you go.

CHRIS (AS STUDENT): Ok. (*Beat*) Hey sir... don't worry about leaving yeah. Good luck at drama school. It's really what you do with it that counts. You'll be amazing.

Chris take in the moment and moves centre stage. CLEARS THE SPACE.

CHRIS: So that's the main task over! Well, turns out the main task is never done. And it's constantly changing. It's a bit of a rolling contract. To live happily ever after? (*Beat*) Next up. (*Beat*) Assessment of Learning: when teachers assess the quality of the learning that has taken place.

My dad's always said 'Life is a learning experience.' He was right... people get heartbroken. Everyday. That's life. (*Beat*) I *felt* like I lost everything. I didn't lose *my* family. But I lost another family. Ryan's.

To live happily ever after. I continued with therapy. I stopped drinking. I started walking. I spent time with those who I loved. I did anything to live more in the present.

And there is a happy ending.

Ryan lives in Australia. We're great friends. Every year he sends my mum and dad a Christmas card. I send one to his. Now that's love, a different type of love. But one I'll happy explain to my kids one day.

> The person will be loved. (*Beat*) Loved from a distance.

Silence.

> A month before going into rehearsal for this show I found some video clips on my computer. Video clips charting years of friends' weddings, building the house and holidays. Some videos I never even knew Ryan had taken. There's one of me and him alone on a beach in Wales. Or rather, just me. The beach is completely empty. The tide is out. I'm in the distance kicking at the sand. It's silent. I'm not making a show or playing up to the camera. It's just me slowly walking in the sand taking in the moment unaware that he's watching. I wonder what he's thinking while he records me. I wonder why he's recorded it.

> And, I met someone else. A new man. A different man. (*Beat*) We were together for a good couple of years. I ended it. And in ending it I learned the responsibility it takes to end it.

Chris takes in the moment. He leans back in his chair and sighs.

> Evaluation. To determine what went well. What did not go well. And what we have learnt for the future.

Chris leans in to the audience.

I'd like to share with you something my dad emailed to me just before I went to drama school. Hilariously, he'd written it six years earlier, a week after running the marathon for the third time. He wrote it, saved it in his draft email folder, forgot about it, and then had the heart attack. He very nearly didn't get to send it at all. (*Beat*)

Lesson's nearly over. Everything ends.

Here's my evaluation.

Chris smiles. The recording plays and Chris exits the space.

26th April, 2006

My darling kids,

I'd like to explain why I ran in the Marathon last Sunday.

I realised as you kids were getting older, you were already facing many of life's tough challenges and during your lifetime you'd be facing many more. Therefore, I feel in attempting to run the 1990 and 1995 Marathon I was demonstrating to you guys, that if we try hard enough to achieve something, we cannot fail. By trying and giving 100% effort we have already succeeded.

After I found my two medals that had been consigned to the loft to gather dust, I decided that

I'd like to give them to my kids. Therefore, as I have three kids I needed to run a third marathon.

I was also aware that by taking on a marathon at the near age of sixty, I would again remind you that we are never too old to try. Please never give up trying whatever it is you want out of life or want to achieve. Life is like the marathon. It's a very long road. Many easy bits. Many hard bits. We sometimes have to pass through the really tough parts and we're likely to learn something about our own character in those tough parts. In the marathon as in life, I also met some wonderful people along the road and we helped each other when help was needed.

I'd also like you three to know that I am immensely happy and proud to have you as my children.

Remember, never ever say *never* and don't forget to call your mother.

Much love

Dad

We Are Family by Sister Sledge begins.

End.